# More Magic Science Tricks

by **DINAH MOCHÉ**

author of
Magic Science Tricks

Cover illustration by Leonard Shortall

Inside illustrations by Richard Rosenblum

## SCHOLASTIC BOOK SERVICES

NEW YORK • TORONTO • LONDON • AUCKLAND • SYDNEY • TOKYO

*For Molly Harrington*

ISBN 0-590-31847-0

Text Copyright © 1980 by Dinah L. Moché. Illustrations copyright © 1980 by Scholastic Magazines Inc. All rights reserved. Published by Scholastic Book Services, a division of Scholastic Magazines, Inc.

12 11 10 9 8 7 6 5 4 3 2 1          10          0 1 2 3 4 5/8

Printed in the U.S.A.                                    02

# More Magic Science Tricks

# Contents

# Magic and Science

Magic and science are both a lot of fun. Some science experiments are so amazing and mysterious that they seem like magic until you understand them. There are 28 easy-to-do science experiments in this book that you can use in a magic show.

Try the experiments first. Then pick out the ones you like best and put on a magic show. Set up a fancy demonstration table, wear a costume, and tell your best jokes. When you've done a trick, you can show what you know by explaining the science behind the trick.

Each experiment has directions that are easy to follow. You will probably find most of the things you need around your home. But if you don't, you can buy what you need at a 5¢ and 10¢ store or a toy-, hobby-, drug-, or hardware store.

## A warning!

Safety is very important in every science laboratory. All the experiments in this book can be performed safely if you follow the directions. Read them through before you start each experiment, and be careful as you work.

When you see one of the symbols below at the beginning of an experiment, turn back to this page and read the special warning.

 Get permission to use the stove. If you don't know how to turn on the stove, ask an adult to help you.

 Be especially careful with matches and candles. Get permission to use them or ask an adult to help you.

 When you are mixing chemicals be very careful not to splash any of the liquid on yourself or on the table where you're working.

Wherever there are safety warnings be sure to pay attention to them.

Now turn the page and have fun.

# Mysterious Tricks

## The Invisible Wall

Put a piece of paper under water without getting it wet.

**You need:** *a paper tissue; a glass; a large bowl; water.*

### The Trick:
Crumple the tissue and push it down firmly in the bottom of the glass. Fill the bowl with water. Turn the glass upside down, then push it straight down into the bowl of water. Make sure the glass is all the way under the water.

Carefully raise the glass straight up out of the water. The paper will be dry.

### The Science:
The glass looks empty, but is full of air. When you push the glass into the water, an invisible wall of air is pushed back against the paper. It keeps the water out and keeps the tissue dry.

# The Tin Can Caper

Blow out a candle that is hidden behind a tin can. (See ✓ page 7.)

**You need:** *a candle in a candle holder; a round can taller than the candle; matches.*

## The Trick:

Light the candle. Put the can in front of the candle. At the level of the flame, blow hard right at the can. The flame will go out.

## The Science:

When your puff of air meets the can, it divides in two. A stream of air races around each side of the can. When the two streams meet again behind the can, they join together and move straight ahead to put out the flame.

Because still air presses harder than moving air, the streams are held close to the sides of the can.

# Super Straw

Push a soda straw into a potato. It will take a little practice, but you can do it.

**You need:** *a raw potato; a soda straw.*

**The Trick:**
Hold the potato in one hand. Hold the straw between the thumb and last three fingers of your other hand. Cover the top of the straw with your index finger. Hold the straw up and plunge it straight into the potato with all your might.

**The Science:**
When you cover the straw with your index finger, you trap air inside. The trapped air makes the straw solid enough to make a hole in the potato.

# The Vanishing Penny

Make a penny disappear without touching it.

**You need:** *a penny; a small clean glass jar with a cover; a small pitcher of water.*

## The Trick:

Put the penny on a table. Set the empty covered jar on top of it. Look at the penny through the side of the jar. Then fill the jar with water and cover it. Look again. The penny will have vanished.

## The Science:

You can see the penny through the empty jar because light rays from the penny go straight to your eyes. You can't see the penny through the jar of water because the water refracts (bends) the light rays upward, away from your eyes.

# Eggs-tra Strong

Balance some heavy books on egg shells without cracking them.

**You need:** *2 uncooked eggs; scissors; 2 or 3 heavy books.*

## The Trick:
Carefully crack the eggs in half in a bowl. Save the insides for cooking and wash off the shells. Use the scissors to straighten the edges of the shells.

Put the shells, open end down, on a table. Arrange them in a rectangle. Set the books right on top of the shells. The shells won't crack.

## The Science:
The fragile shells don't crack under the weight of the books because of their domed shape. The weight of the books is spread out over the whole curved surface of each shell. It doesn't just rest on one spot. Domes are used in building construction—from igloos to the Astrodome — because of their great strength.

# Believe It or Not

## A Tumbling Act

Without tilting, tipping, or touching, you can make some buttons bounce around in a glass. (See page 7.)

**You need:** *a glass of water; vinegar; baking soda; a tablespoon; 3 to 5 tiny buttons.*

**The Trick:**
Add 4 tablespoons of vinegar to the glass of water. Stir in 3 tablespoons of baking soda. Bubbles will begin to form.

Drop the buttons into the glass. They will fall to the bottom of the glass — but then they will begin to rise. When they reach the top of the liquid, they will tumble back down — then rise again.

**The Science:**
The vinegar and baking soda combine to make carbon dioxide gas. When the bubbles of carbon dioxide collect on the buttons they carry them to the top. At the top of the liquid the bubbles pop and the buttons sink again. When new bubbles collect, the buttons will rise again.

# Tiger Tamer

Be a tiger tamer. Get the tiger into the cage.

**You need:** *index card 3 by 5 inches; crayons; a piece of string about 12 inches long; scissors.*

## The Trick:
Draw a cage on one side of the index card. On the other side of the card, draw a tiger small enough to fit into the cage. (You can trace the one on the next page.)

Cut the string in half. Make a hole on each side of the card—halfway down from the top. Thread a piece of string through each hole and knot it.

Hold the strings straight out from the sides of the card. Twirl the strings between your fingers so the card flips over and over rapidly. You will see the tiger inside the cage.

## The Science:
When you look at a picture the image forms on the retina of your eye. It stays there for about 1/16 of a second—even if the picture is taken away. Then the image goes to your brain and you see the picture.

If a new picture is placed in front of your eyes before the image of the first one gets to your brain, you'll see a combination of the two pictures.

# Paper Magic

Cut a strip of paper in half and still have just one piece of paper.

**You need:** *a piece of paper about 1 inch by 11 inches; glue; pencil; scissors.*

## The Trick:

Give one end of the strip of paper a half-twist. Then glue the ends together so that you have a loop.

Starting anywhere on the strip, draw a line down the center of the paper. Cut along the pencil line. The strip will stay in one piece.

## The Science:

This paper strip has just one side. It is called a Moebius strip after the mathematician who discovered it. Mathematicians are interested in surfaces with just one side because they are so unusual.

If you glue the ends of a strip of paper together to make an ordinary ring, a line drawn around the outside of the ring will never go inside. If you cut along the line, you will get two separate rings.

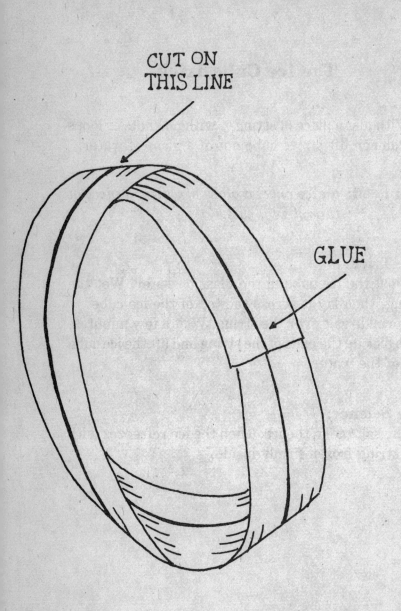

CUT ON
THIS LINE

GLUE

# The Ice Cube Trick

With just a piece of string—with no knots or loops—you can lift an ice cube out of a glass of water.

**You need:** *an ice cube; a glass of water; a piece of thin string; salt.*

**The Trick:**
Float the ice cube in the glass of water. Wet the string, then lay it across the top of the ice cube.

Sprinkle salt over the string. Wait a few minutes, then pick up the ends of the string and lift the ice cube out of the water.

**The Science:**
The salt melts the ice. Then the ice refreezes with the string frozen firmly inside.

# Battle of the Balloons

Which is mightier? The big balloon or the little balloon?

**You need:** *2 balloons (9-inch size or larger); 2 twist ties; a spool.*

## Setting up the trick:

Blow one balloon up all the way. Then tie the neck of the balloon tightly with a twist tie so air can't escape. Stretch the opening of the balloon over one end of the spool.

Blow up the other balloon about half way. Tie it tightly, then stretch the opening over the other end of the spool.

## The Trick:

Untie the small balloon. As long as one of the balloons is tied, air can't escape from either balloon.

Now untie the big balloon. You would expect air to rush from the big balloon into the small balloon. But just the opposite happens. Air rushes from the small balloon into the big balloon.

## The Science:

The air in the small balloon is more crowded than the air in the big balloon. So the pressure is greater in the small balloon. When the big balloon is untied, air from the small balloon is pushed into the big balloon.

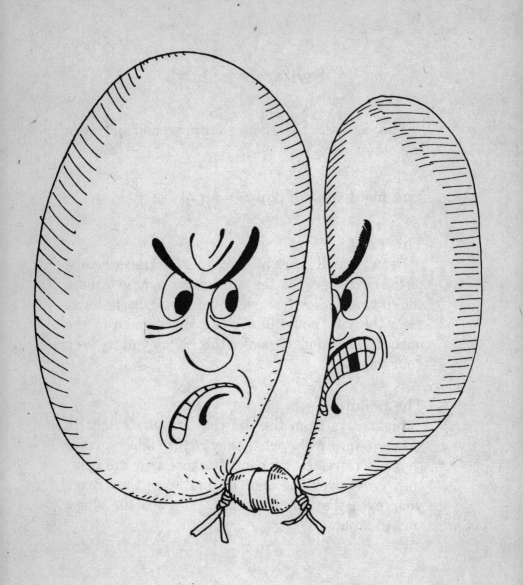

# Swimming Shark

You can order this shark to turn around and swim the other way.

**You need:** *pencil; paper; a jar of water.*

## The Trick:
Draw a small shark on the paper, or trace the one on the next page. Put the jar of water right in front of the drawing. Slowly move the drawing back, away from the jar. You will see the shark swim in the opposite direction. (Practice this before you try it on your friends.)

## The Science:
Light rays from the drawing travel straight to your eyes in air. But when they go through the water they are refracted, or bent. Because they are bent, they cross over one another and when they reach your eyes they are reversed. You see the shark turned around.

# Crime Detection

## Fingerprinting

You can make your own fingerprint file.

**You need:** *a no. 2 pencil; a piece of paper; sticky transparent tape; white index cards; a file box.*

**The Trick:**
Start with your own fingerprint. Write your name at the top of an index card. Tear off a piece of sticky tape and lay it, sticky side up, on a table. With the pencil, make a black smudge on the piece of paper. Rub your thumb over the smudge, then press it down firmly on the sticky tape.

Wipe off your thumb, then stick the tape down on the index card. You'll have a clear image of your thumbprint. (You can make prints this way of all your friends.)

**The Science:**
No two people have the same pattern of ridges on their fingertips—not even identical twins. Therefore fingerprints can help identify people. Whenever you handle something you leave a fingerprint — smudging the fingertip makes the print easier to see.

# Lifting Fingerprints

If you want to find out whose greasy fingerprint is on the silverware, here's how.

**You need:** *a soup spoon with a fresh greasy fingerprint; talcum powder; a small paintbrush; sticky tape; a piece of black paper; magnifying glass; your fingerprint file (see page 30).*

## The Trick:

Try this on yourself first. Put a *little* grease on your thumb, then press it on the bowl of the spoon.

Sprinkle talcum powder lightly over the fingerprint. Gently brush the powder so that it sticks to the fingerprint. Blow away any extra powder.

Carefully press a piece of sticky tape over the fingerprint. Rub over the surface of the tape gently so the powder will stick to it. Lift the tape and stick it down on the black paper. Match the fingerprint with one of those in your file box.

## The Science:

Talcum powder sticks to the fingerprint while it is fresh. A fresh non-greasy fingerprint is practically all water and it dries out fast. The FBI uses iodine vapor to develop fingerprints left at the scene of a crime. But they too must act quickly and carefully.

# Counterfeit Coin Collector

Separate real money from slugs.

**You need:** *a strong horseshoe magnet; sticky tape; a thin gift box with cover; a piece of cardboard the same size as the bottom of the box; a pencil; ruler; scissors; coins; several steel washers.*

### Making the Coin Collector:

Draw a straight line across the middle of the piece of the cardboard on the front and the back. Tape the magnet to the cardboard so that the "poles" (ends) of the magnet are touching the line. Fit the cardboard, with the magnet side down, in the bottom of the box.

Cut a slot one-inch wide on each side of the box just where the pencil line on the cardboard meets the sides of the box. Then cover the box.

### The Trick:

Tilt the box and slip a coin through the top slot. The coin will slide down the line and come out the bottom slot. Now try a washer. It won't come out. It will stick to the magnet.

## The Science:

Some metals—such as iron (which is used in steel)—are strongly attracted by magnets. Other metals—such as copper, which is used in making nickels, dimes, quarters, and pennies—are not attracted by magnets.

Vending machines make use of magnets to separate slugs from coins.

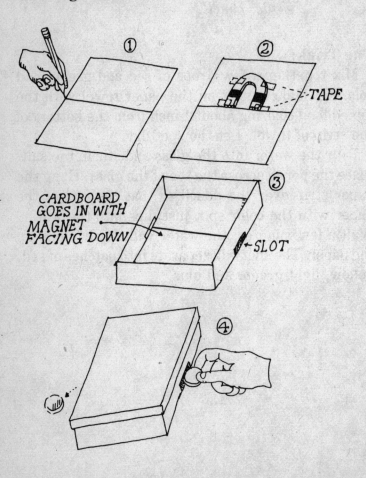

① 

② ←TAPE

③

CARDBOARD GOES IN WITH MAGNET FACING DOWN

←SLOT

④

# Chemical Test

Separate chemicals in your crime lab.

**You need:** *a clean glass; ¼ cup of water; teaspoon of salt; green and red liquid food coloring; a strip of paper towel about 1-inch wide; pencil.*

**The Trick:**
Mix together a few drops of red and green food coloring. Make a spot on the paper towel with the mixed food coloring about 1 inch from the bottom of the strip of towel. Let the spot dry.

Pour the water into the glass and stir in the salt. Place the pencil across the top of the glass. Hang the paper strip over the pencil so that the end of the paper with the color spot just dips into the water. Wait a few minutes, the water will slowly climb up the paper. The spot will separate into patches of red, yellow, light green, and blue.

**The Science:**

The food coloring is a mixture of different colored chemicals. As the salt water climbs up the paper, it dissolves the chemicals. Some chemicals rise higher than others. Separating chemicals this way is called *chromatography*, which means "write with colors." When the chemicals are separated they can be identified.

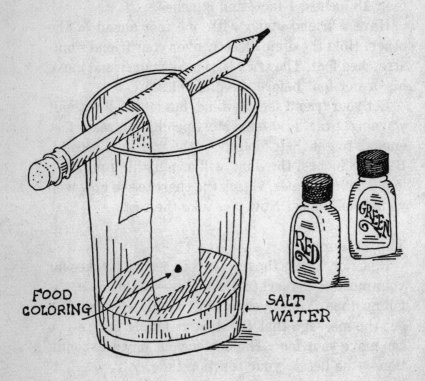

FOOD COLORING

SALT WATER

RED

GREEN

# Mind Over Body

## Reaction Time

Try this test on your friends. See how fast they react.

**You need:** *a yardstick; a dime.*

**The Trick:**
The chart on the next page shows how long it normally takes for a dime to fall to the ground from 4 feet, 18 inches, 1 foot, and 8 inches.

Have a friend stand with one foot ahead of the other. Hold the dime directly over your friend's outstretched foot. The trick is to have your friend move his or her foot before the dime hits it.

Let your friend see the dime, but let it fall without warning. Start at 4 feet. Most people can react fast enough to get their foot out of the way in ½ second. But at 8 inches, the dime will usually hit a person's foot 2 out of 3 times. Check the chart to see how well your friend does. Now you take the test.

**The Science:**
Reaction time is the fraction of a second it takes for your muscles to react to a stimulus—in this case, the falling dime. Your eyes, brain, and muscles must all get the message that the dime is falling before you can move your foot. The better your physical condition—the better your reaction time.

DIME FALLS

4 FEET IN ½ SECOND

18 INCHES IN ⅓ SECOND

1 FOOT IN ¼ SECOND

8 INCHES IN ⅕ SECOND

# A Steady Hand

Do you have a steady hand? Test yourself.

**You need:** *hobby battery; 40 inches of thin bare copper wire; 45 inches of bell wire; flashlight bulb in socket; shoebox with cover; scissors; tape; glue; small screwdriver.*

## Setting up the Trick:

Glue the socket on one end of the box top. Make a tiny hole next to the socket. Make 2 tiny holes in the other end of the box top.

Shape the copper wire like the bumpy track of a roller coaster. Then connect one end of the wire to one of the screws on the socket, by wrapping it around the screw. (Use the screwdriver to loosen and tighten the screws.) Push the other end of the copper wire through one of the holes in the other end of the box top. Tape it securely to the inside of the box top.

Put the battery inside the box. (When the box is closed the battery and the socket should be on the same side of the box.)

Cut 2 pieces of bell wire: one piece 15 inches long and one piece 30 inches long. Remove 1 inch of the covering (insulation) from both ends of each wire. Connect one end of each wire to the screws on the battery.

Push the 15-inch wire through the hole near the socket. Connect it to one of the screws on the socket. Pull the 30-inch wire through the remaining hole at the other end of the box top. Put the top on the box.

## The Trick:

Make a small loop around the bumpy roller-coaster track with the end of the 30-inch wire. See if your hand is steady enough to move the loop over the track without making the light go on. When you finish the test, open the loop so the light doesn't stay on and use up the battery.

## The Science:

The bulb lights up when electricity flows through it. Electricity can only flow from the battery to the bulb if it has a complete path, or circuit. When you touch the loop to the wire track you complete the circuit.

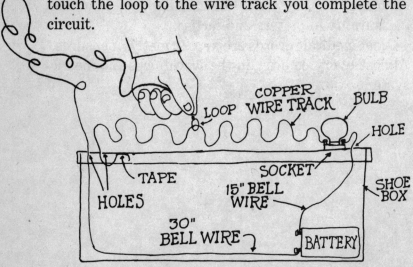

# Your Metric Measure

How tall are you—in meters? Find out with your own metric tape measure.

**You need:** *a 40-inch strip of strong plastic (from an old window shade or tablecloth); a pen.*

**What to do:**
Use the metric ruler on the next page as a guide. Put the plastic strip next to the ruler and mark off the lines. The ruler is 10 centimeters long. There are 100 centimeters in one meter. And 10 millimeters in one centimeter. If you are 4 feet tall, you are 1.2 meters tall.

On the back of your metric measure you can mark off inches so that you'll know at a glance how you measure up in meters and inches.

Most medical records are kept in metric measures. Almost every country in the world uses the metric system.

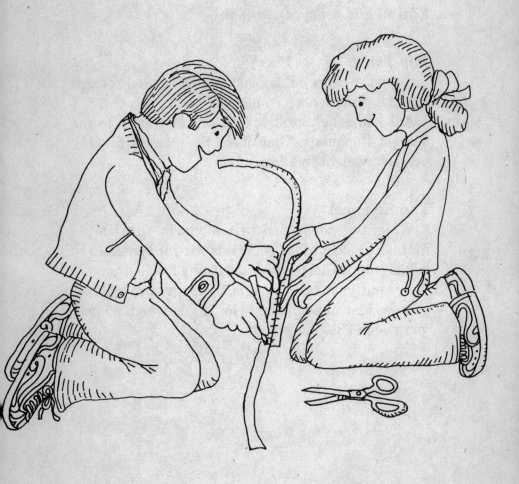

# What's Your Metric Weight?

Amaze your family and friends by telling their weight in kilograms without a metric scale.

**You need:** *pencil; index card.*

**The Trick:**
Copy the chart on the next page on an index card. Put the chart where no one can see it.

Ask someone to tell you his or her weight to the nearest 10 pounds. Then check the chart to find the person's weight in kilograms.

**The Science:**
Weight is measured in pounds in the United States. In most other countries weight is measured in kilograms. One pound is almost half a kilogram. To figure out your *exact* weight in kilograms, multiply your weight in pounds by .45. If you weigh 85 lbs., you weigh 38¼ kilograms.

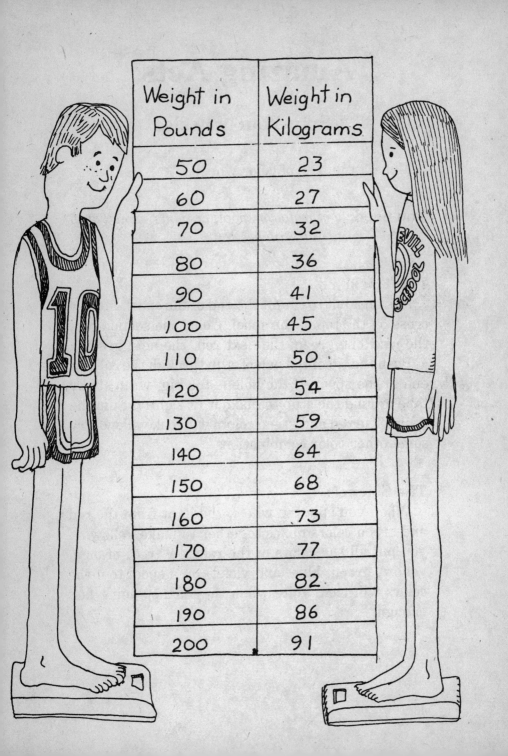

| Weight in Pounds | Weight in Kilograms |
|:---:|:---:|
| 50 | 23 |
| 60 | 27 |
| 70 | 32 |
| 80 | 36 |
| 90 | 41 |
| 100 | 45 |
| 110 | 50 |
| 120 | 54 |
| 130 | 59 |
| 140 | 64 |
| 150 | 68 |
| 160 | 73 |
| 170 | 77 |
| 180 | 82 |
| 190 | 86 |
| 200 | 91 |

# Amazing Acts

## Spin Your Wheels

Make a rainbow of color wheels.

**You need:** *a styrofoam spool; crayons; pencil stub about 2 inches long.*

**The Trick:**
Ask an adult to cut off the end of the spool. Make a cross on the top of the spool. Color one section red, the next one green, the next red, the next green.

Push the tip of the pencil stub through the colored end of the spool. If the hole is too big, wrap sticky tape around the stub to make it fit tightly. Spin the spool. The red and green colors will look yellow. Try some other color combinations.

**The Science:**
When you spin the wheel, the light from the red and green colors mixes together to make yellow. If you put all the colors of the rainbow (red, orange, yellow, green, blue, and violet) on a spool top, the colors will look white when they are spinning fast enough.

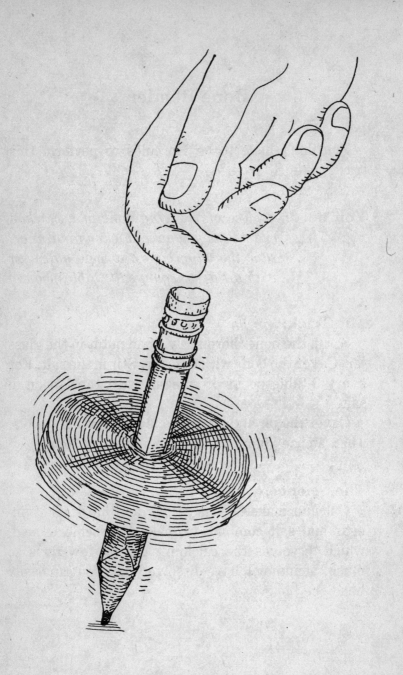

# Bone Bender

You don't have to be Hercules to perform this trick! (See 🧪 page 7.)

**You need:** *a piece of the wing bone of a chicken (next time you have chicken for dinner, save the wing bone); a wide glass jar with a lid; vinegar; salt; tablespoon.*

### The Trick:

Scrub the bone thoroughly, then put it in the glass jar. Cover the bone with vinegar. Stir in the salt. For every 3 tablespoons of vinegar use 1 tablespoon of salt.

Cover the jar and let the bone soak for a few days. Then amaze your friends by bending the bone.

### The Science:

Calcium makes bones strong and hard. The vinegar and salt combine to make hydrochloric acid, which dissolves the calcium. After a few days so much calcium will have dissolved that you can easily bend the bone.

# Roller Box

No gas, no wheels in this roller derby.

**You need:** *an empty oatmeal box with cover; a strong rubber band; a heavy metal nut; a nail; a twist tie; 2 large paper clips.*

## Making the Roller Box:
Use the nail to make a hole in the center of the cover and the bottom of the box. Slip the rubber band through the nut and tie the band tightly around the nut. Slip one end of the rubber band through the hole in the bottom of the box and slide a paper clip through the loop in the rubber band.

Use the twist tie to pull the other end of the rubber band up through the hole in the cover. Secure the rubber band with the other paper clip. Fit the cover on the box.

## The Trick:
Roll the box away from you on a bare floor. It will roll back to you.

## The Science:
The rubber band winds up when you roll the box away from you. Energy is stored in the coiled rubber band. This stored energy drives the box back to you.

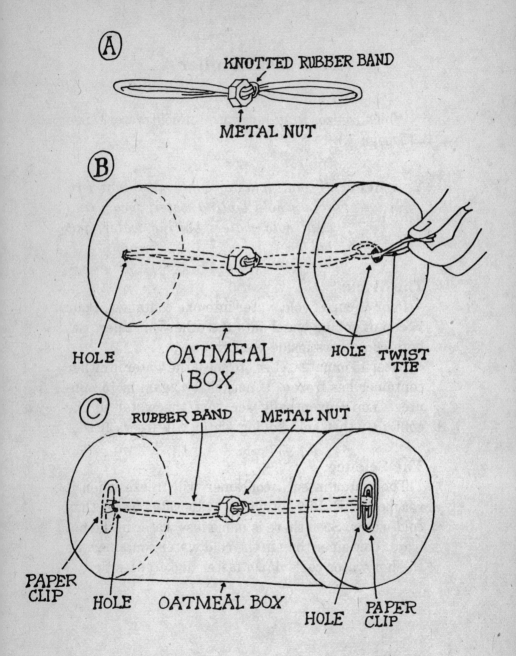

(A) KNOTTED RUBBER BAND
METAL NUT

(B) HOLE
OATMEAL BOX
HOLE   TWIST TIE

(C) RUBBER BAND   METAL NUT
PAPER CLIP
HOLE   OATMEAL BOX
HOLE   PAPER CLIP

# A Real Chiller

Which freezes first: hot water or cold water? (See page 7.)

**You need:** *2 small plastic containers that can safely hold boiling water; measuring cup; cold water; boiling water; pot holder.*

## The Trick:

Pour ½ cup of cold water into one container. Pour ½ cup of boiling water into the other container. Set both containers inside your freezer.

After 45 minutes, check to see if the water in either container has frozen. If not, check again in 15 minutes. You'll eventually see that the water in the container that held boiling water will freeze first.

## The Science:

The water in each container will freeze when it reaches 32°F. But hot water evaporates faster than cold water. Soon there is much less water in the hot water container than in the cold water container. So the hot water cools down faster and freezes first.

# Rolling Uphill

This funnel-car seems to defy gravity by rolling uphill.

**You need:** *2 plastic funnels; glue; 2 pieces of cardboard 14 inches by 1½ inches; several books.*

## Making the funnel-car and track:

Glue the rims of the funnels together. Let the glue set. Glue the strips of cardboard together at one end. Spread the cardboard to make a V. This is your track.

## The Trick:

Pile two stacks of books — one a little higher than the other. Rest the point of the track on the short pile and the legs of the track on the higher pile.

Put the funnel-car on the lower end of the track. The stems should rest on the track. Now the funnel-car will roll to the top of the track.

## The Science:

The funnel-car only appears to roll uphill. Nothing can roll uphill by itself because gravity pulls everything down. Watch the funnel-car from the side as it rolls. You'll see that as the track gets wider and wider, the center of the funnel-car gets lower and lower. It is really rolling downhill.

# Things To Make

## Snowstorm in a Jar

**You need:** *a small wide-mouthed glass jar with a screw-on cover; some tiny plastic figures; waterproof glue; 2 hard-boiled eggs; water; a teaspoon of salt.*

Arrange the plastic figures in an interesting scene on the inside of the cover of the jar. Then glue the figures in place.

Peel the eggs and crush the shells into tiny bits. (Save the eggs for lunch.) Fill the jar with water and then stir in the salt.

Put the crushed eggshells in the jar. Screw the cap, with the plastic figures, on the jar. Make sure it fits tightly.

To start the snowstorm, turn the jar upside down.

# Rock Candy

**You need:** *a clean 8-ounce glass; a cup of water; pot holder; 2 cups of granulated sugar; wooden spoon; small saucepan; piece of thin clean string; a pencil.*

Bring the cup of water to a boil in the saucepan. (See ⬚ page 7.) Turn off the heat. Add the sugar. Stir with the wooden spoon until all the sugar is dissolved. Set the pan aside and let the sugar solution cool.

Tie the string around the middle of the pencil. Rest the pencil on top of the glass and let the string hang into the glass, almost to the bottom.

Pour the cooled sugar solution into the glass. Set the glass in a warm place where no one will disturb it for a few days.

Soon sugar crystals will begin to form on the string. When a crust forms on top of the water, break it. More sugar crystals (rock candy) will grow on the string. Pick off the crystals and eat them.

# Homemade Planetarium

**You need:** *an empty oatmeal box with several extra tops; several sheets of tracing paper; pencil; scissors; nail; sticky tape; a flashlight; black construction paper.*

Trace one of the star patterns on the next page on a piece of paper. Tape the paper down on the outside of one of the box tops. With the nail, make holes through the box top at each star. Make a different star pattern for each box top.

Cut a hole in the bottom of the box big enough to slip the flashlight through. Cover the shiny reflector of the flashlight with black construction paper.

When you are ready to give a star show, put one of the tops on the box. Slip the flashlight into the box. Make sure the room is dark. Turn on the flashlight. Shine the star pattern onto the ceiling.

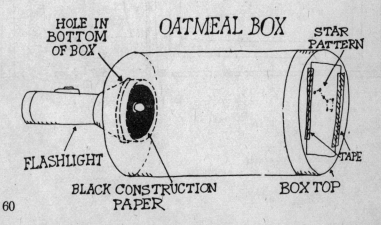

HOLE IN BOTTOM OF BOX

OATMEAL BOX

STAR PATTERN

FLASHLIGHT

BLACK CONSTRUCTION PAPER

TAPE

BOX TOP

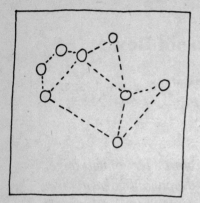

SAGITTARIUS THE ARCHER

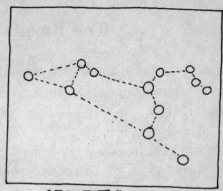

LEO THE LION

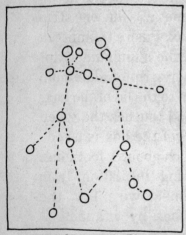

GEMINI THE TWINS

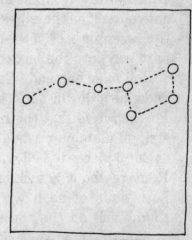

THE BIG DIPPER

# The Burglar-Proof Box

Make a burglar-proof box for your most secret possessions.

**You need:** *a hobby battery; about 3 feet of bell wire; an electric bell; a disposable aluminum baking pan; 2 thumbtacks; small screwdriver; cigar box; glue; scissors.*

Cut 2 strips of aluminum—about 3 inches long and 1-inch wide—from the baking pan. (Be careful not to cut yourself on the edges of the metal.) Glue one strip to the center back of the cigar box. Push a thumbtack part way into the box through the aluminum strip.

Roll over one end of the other strip of aluminum and glue it down. Tack this strip to the lid of the box. Position it so that the rolled end touches the glued strip of aluminum when the lid of the box is lifted.

Cut 3 pieces of bell wire—each about 1-foot long. Remove about ½ inch of covering (insulation) from both ends of each wire. Connect wire 1 to the thumbtack on the top of the box by wrapping it around the thumbtack. Then connect the other end to one of the screws on the battery.

Connect wire 2 to the other battery screw and one of the screws on the bell. Connect wire 3 to the other screw on the bell and the thumbtack on the back of the box. Use the screwdriver to loosen and tighten the screws on the bell.

Lift the lid, the bell will ring. When the aluminum strips touch, electricity has a closed metal path (circuit) to flow through.

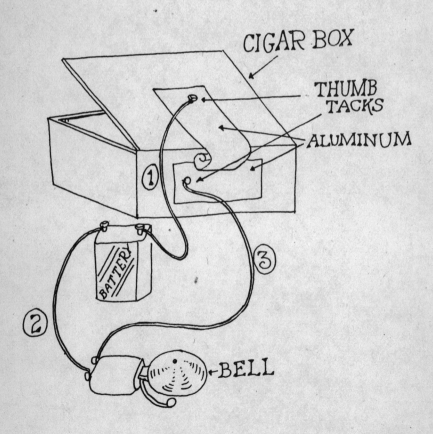

CIGAR BOX

THUMB TACKS

ALUMINUM

BATTERY

←BELL